MW00760327

GIRL TORPEDO

Emari DiGiorgio

Published by Agape Editions
http://agapeeditions.com
Los Angeles, CA

Copyright © 2018 by Emari DiGiorgio
All rights reserved

This title was selected by Allison Joseph as recipient of the 2017
Numinous Orisons, Luminous Origin Literary Award for Poetry.

Cover image: Girl Torpedo
Artist: Mandy Heck
Image is used here by kind permission of the artist.

Cover & interior design: De Anna Ienopoli & Jasmine An

Editors: Jasmine An & Fox Frazier-Foley

Agape Editions titles are printed using Lightning Source
and distributed by Ingram Content Group.

This title is also for purchase directly from the publisher.

Library of Congress
Cataloguing-in-Publication Data
Girl Torpedo // Emari DiGiorgio
Library of Congress Control Number 2017953478

DiGiorgio, Emari
ISBN 978-1-939675-62-0

9 8 7 6 5 4 3 2 1

AGAPE
EDITIONS

for Syra, who asked me to sing and taught me to love my voice

CONTENTS

4

1

PLAYING THE HUSBAND

When you were the husband, you kissed up my back,
lips cresting each ridge of spine. When I was the husband,

I traced your name—the only poem I knew—
with pointer finger, then tongue, in the small frame

your shoulder blades made. When you were the husband,
I lay flat on my back and closed my eyes. When I closed

my eyes, the room didn't smell like musty blankets, damp
weather, strawberry shampoo. When you were the husband,

I couldn't be the husband. When you were the wife,
I wanted to be the wife. When you licked my wrist,

I imagined I was someplace I wasn't supposed to be.
When I was the wife, I never asked how you learned to be

the husband; the wife doesn't ask questions. When you
taught me how to be the husband, you instructed through

touch, the room dark. *Hold me like this.* When we stripped,
I had this extra gene called inhibition. Once, when you

were the husband, I told you to stop. No one taught me
to be the wife. You never cried. You never wanted me to stop.

LITTLE BLACK DRESS

Cut above-the-knee with shoulder straps
at least two-fingers thick, scoop neck,
slight cinch at waist, fabric that drapes.
I'm not going to blame myself or this

dress, its little floral filigree. Not a cape
to be twirled in a frat house's black light
to rile the bull, to make him want blood.
That animal who gored me is a man,

not some 1600lb beast with a banderilla
in his back. This dress is dead. Pull it
over my head and we'll burst into flame.
Instead of a sabre through his ticker, I want

him to eat the evidence with his hands,
a Coney Island dress-eating contest, stuffing
dry strips of cloth in his mouth, or dipping
them in lemonade, which turns pink or brown

from whatever's confined in the fibers. This
isn't a timed competition. Every day, he'll eat
the same dress. Every day, he'll taste me
and what he did to me. Every day, he'll gag

on the tag, the small band of elastic. His one
meal because he wanted it so bad. Meanwhile
in the precinct basement, all of the clothing
locked up as evidence—jogging shorts, flannel

pajamas, cardigans, scrubs—thrash in a circle
pit, unfurling empty sleeves, so much rage
and shame to stomp, to peel from concrete
floor, to hold up to the room's caged light.

UN-NAMING A THING

Limbs pinned or   under attack, stiff   a little dizzy,
slack, body relaxed,   hard smack Darkness   language escaping,

the word *no,* its   *now, I don't know,*   And if he doesn't?
siblings: *not right*   *wait, please, stop*   Some ventriloquy

mouth moving,   my back the mime   or bound or I am
not my hand   itself not gagged   figuratively

The room's twin   A little nervous   where something
beds, not mine, his?   laughter A burp   comes up and

I swallow the whole   betrays me Was I   I go limp, hands
incident—the body   able to fight or did   gripping coverlet,

tearing flesh   the scarlet V   in not naming
I don't want to wear   there's something   an act What else

to call it?   Whereas rape is   nonconsensual sex
And if he stopped?   three-minutes or more   Whereas there was

digital penetration   unwanted penetration   Husk of a girl
of the vagina and/or   by the penis   corn-silk hair

fanned on the bed   I didn't say no,   ready I said I wasn't
still clothed,   but I said I wasn't   ready And it was

as if he'd taken   revealing triple   lemons a horseshoe
a nickel to my silver   sevens rotten cherries   upside down

WHERE MERMAIDS COME FROM

Her nicked torso gives way to thighs bound
by iridescent scales, a tiled roof
that shimmers in rain, slick and dangerous.
No feet but a tail, split, a serpent's tongue
to lick or lap water at shore's edge.
She's still a she, but harder to pin down.

Folks with fanny packs and visors down
for holiday avoid seedy motels bound
by bay and intercostal waterway. Dandelions edge
four lowercase-t crosses. The Starlight's roof
half open to sky. Low tide's tongue
streaks gray-green muck dangerous:

a plastic worm with hidden hook. Danger's
gaze, that strain to look composed when down
on luck. Bloodshot eyes betray tongue,
No, I'm fine. I've found myself bound
by my sex too—flashflood, trapped on roof;
a woman idling night's addled edges.

Close enough to see ribs stretch, hear edge
of breath? Her light eyes: dangerous,
like stars collapsing in on themselves.
My want to be sexless and without desire down-
played in case it comes true. She isn't bound
to this place now, fluent in the tongue

of Atlantic's whorling deep. Casinos tongue
the horizon to the east. My only edge—
stench of tidal bodies' bound
promise—return at dusk, danger's
hour, hoist her on a tarp I've wet down,
so skin won't stick or tear, and roofed

by car, we'll steal through town, roofs
aglow, until we reach island's tongue:
a straight shot to sea. I down
bilious envy, ask *what's at the edge?*
She shakes her head, detached, as if danger's
lease has snapped. The throwaway girl's unbound—

left shoeless in roofless marsh, moon edging
split lip, swollen tongue, the dangerous hum of a girl
down, bound, strangled with a bit of hose.

BED OF NAILS

I, too, have learned
to distribute my weight

so that no separate
point pricks, have lain

so still, tried to disappear,
when a man, who said

the magic words *I love you,*
pulled the small dove

of his prick in and out,
as if I were some silk hat.

ON THE CAVE WALL, THE GREAT BLACK BIRD
CARRIES A GIRL INTO THE SKY

Whatever the boy had done to her, we'll never know.
It was just this once, or it wasn't. When he returned
to the village, how could he explain her absence—

who hadn't noticed the way he looked at her—
and it was no secret that they'd walked off together
earlier in the afternoon. How to explain how everything

pulsed within him and how she turned away,
dismissing his ardor splayed at river's edge. And so,
he blamed that tiger of the sky: the one they'd all seen

knock a Gaur—three times its size—dead, with one
soundless blow. The boy stood with sunset bleeding
into horizon, told how bird drove girl aground,

how her eyes rolled back, like transparent eggs,
and how immediately sand soaked red around,
and as he took a step toward her, it sank talons

into pelvis, carried her away: the story becoming
more real as he told it. And he ran through jungle,
at first following the shadowed wingspan, which

quickly outpaced him, and then drops of blood,
which fell as fast as his tears, and he stopped
only at cliff's lip where he sobbed. People gathered

and sharpened spears. *The girl was gone.* Elders
painted the wall. The boy had been so brave.
They'd clip its monstrous wings, set its entrails ablaze.

Women and children wept; hunters raided its nest,
cooked its eggs, set traps, and beat the bird to death.
For weeks, they cut open each eagle's belly, half

waiting for the girl to emerge whole. Soon the bird
began to pluck elders gathering herbs and children
from fields. The boy, now a man, dreams of the girl

by the river, how he held her under until she sank,
how she surfaces—cedar-stained, bald, with bulging
eyes—to press her swollen black lips to his own.

WHERE DOES THE RABBIT GO WHEN THE HOUNDS ARE LOOSED?

From where does the haunting rise, the perennial feeling
in the gut? Where are all the male teachers who kissed

and touched the just graduated or the ones still students?
Where's the prom queen's acceptance speech so thankful

for getting to know Principal Such & Such? Where's his
pregnant wife? Where's my sixteen-year-old body?

Where are spin and fall? Where does a girl torpedo strike
an old battleship? Where's the love she wants? Where are

the boys who don't have a clue? Where are the grown men
who know better? Where's consequence? And Monica?

Where's the scandal with his last name? Where did she go
down on him because she didn't want to have sex?

Where am I not guilty of that, so guilty, I got good at it?
Where have I not been touched? Where is each he who

thought suck and swallow were gifts? Where's my pretty
young thing? Where's the man who doesn't want to own me?

THE JINXED BULLET CATCH

after Dorothy Dietrich

The air's a sheet cake.
She's as ready as she's ever been, this lady waiting, a woman
in white fringe, angel face, a witch's uneven hem.

     The marksman takes aim,
     double-paned glass—crowd gasp—
     the small black crevasse.

What stops her knees from buckling?
                         5   4   3   2   1   and the gun.

The crack, slap, and shattered glass, her own foot kicking out
the window of her bedroom the last time her father
brought the belt.

        How many threats has she already swallowed?
        This woman without a ballistics expert,
        her homemade mouthpiece to catch the bullet—

.22 caliber jewel of naught   little death scarab   unswallowed pill—

        sparing uvula's guillotine. The trick: to soften
        the throat, the way you might take a ball into a mitt.

I'm sixteen on the third base line
when coach calls my name, drives a line drive
to the bridge of my nose. Cartilage inverts,

        sinus bones split, a wash of blood
        rushes from the two pig holes above my lips,
        staining shirt, glove, gravel at my feet.

What to do but try to hold yourself upright.
               A girl's used to holding her face like this.

WHEN I WAS THE DIVING GIRL

The best of us were used to falling,
      had learned how to cling
        to the back and neck of beasts,
men who thrashed at the bottom of their own

dark pools. I was a swim-slick marvel,
      the oils of my make-up intact,
Atlantic City's circus act, five dollars a show.
      All summer—flashbulbs split open sky.

The day's last jump: crowd hushed,
expectant, and I, a bride, knock-kneed,
      shivering, at what was to come.
      Forty feet below, the water,

      a desilvered old mirror, darkest at center.
How easy to forget to close my eyes,
everything slowing to a waltz, my face
      stretched against wind, until

a hoof steps in. Then cheers: the pier's
      martini sloshing off the boards,
a thousand pounds of water displaced.
A few wait to be sure I resurface

intact, pry for a crack in my smile,
      a limp. Perhaps the payoff's
      worth the threat:
           I'd get to do it over again.

THE WHITE HORSES OF WAINUI BEACH

I've felt the dredging stride, a hoof
upon my chest or back. To slide along
their slick coats before they buck and rear—

a circus act. No trainer walks these steeds.
The wet sand sinks beneath the weight
of the white water's muscled flanks.

Only moon-spooked, not gods or demons,
with calla-white manes. They run themselves
aground and vanish in the foam as if

tethered to the plow of the sea. I, too,
am bound to this earth and wish to know
what it is to shatter and resurface whole.

2

WHO HASN'T HOARDED ONE MILKY STONE IN A DEEP POCKET?

I've given up many things to the elements:
that floor-length red leather trench, my father's violin.
When the storm rolls in, it's hard to quiet the crew

in my veins, all of them asking how far until shore,
and I'm the type of Captain who wants everyone
to have a say. Suddenly, I've let the lifeboats go.

Suddenly, I'm alone in a maelstrom with one hand
on the rudder, one on my heart, inventing a pledge
of allegiance, as I replay the surveillance tape of my brain.

❦

When the man asks for water, I hesitate: part of me
wants to offer and the other doesn't say a thing.
It's on my tongue, even after he leaves, in a white car

with two of our bags. Let's just pretend it was something
that couldn't be avoided, that it was a fire, not a theft
disguised as a friendly face who's stopped to fix your flat.

❦

Here's where they knifed the back tire—a steady leak,
a sure tear, thirty minutes from the airport. Here's
where the lug nuts come loose. The man talks

and squawks and kicks up gravel like a peacock.
While we watch his silver grill flash—presto—
money, passports, laptop vamoose from the cab.

The man waves a gun in my face; there's
a skirmish, blood and light streak upholstered seats.
My fair-haired daughter disappears.

⁓

This backwards spinning reel, this light recast, this
other version, as up to chance as the last. I'd trade
the bags for the girl, the splinters of my craft—

a sheaf of loose-leaf drafts, handwritten journals,
stanza and paragraph, line and rhyme—stretched
across the shore and floating back to sea.

ODE TO AFTERTHOUGHT

What might have been useful before
especially if money or concrete or surgery

was involved. Dry wood after the fire's snuffed out.
Some conditional. A salve to ease word's burn.

The tribe of retaliation, upright on horses
just crossing the stream, moving with the seasons.

When I think, whole continents can collide
or unstick in the brain. But what's beyond?

The thing that sets off flares, when some mouth
wedged between my ribs says *Go, now.*

Thought rides in on its horse. Or it's a foot soldier.
Sometimes my flag bearer makes it to the next leg

of the journey, builds the Trojan horse, the idea
of Helen, the catapult. Was ego or victory so loud

it drowned out my voice, yours, which of us said,
I don't know about this?

TODDLER PULLED FROM RUBBLE IN ALEPPO

What comfort in dark of collapse: dry womb,
throb of ambulance heartbeat. Two minutes,
twelve seconds to pluck the girl from stone:

a small trophy the men lift to camera. In her crib,
my child sleeps: stone cut from bones; a mother's
love, an axe. To believe this roof won't collapse,

I build a storied fortress, a fiction my privilege
enacts. My share of calamity's minute but inflated—
hot air balloon building heat, speed, so far above

those ground-bound, digging barehanded through
stone. Sirens rattle: war's ragged heart beats
in 4/4 time, passed down until a heart beats still.

To survive or thrive: the distance between
two buildings, which end of axe in hand.

THIS HAMMER I'VE INHERITED

Heavy tool at my belt,
no good at fixing
a broken canine
or a cavity, treating
cancer, making sure
the water's clean,
can't fix a rising tide/
low floodplain,
a high ball already
cracked; ancient tool,
made at home with sticks
and stones a length
of twine—always
the girl quick to strike
with my mouth, told
a boy at least I don't
live in a hand-me-down
house, no I lived
in a ranch house haunted
by a child ghost and
black mold, where
backhands were served
more often than side salads
at dinner, oh, I can be
cruel and good at wrecking
spirits, have struck down
with judgment, held
a grudge two lifetimes,
yelled war instead
of peace, feigned
the stigmata, left
a two-toed print in sand
and snow to spook
the soft-bodied creatures;

I've taken a bridge,
removed the nails, stolen
all the other hammers too;
a hammer's good
for busting holes
in drywall, old tile,
removing a rusty
hinge, but even then,
I've missed many times,
smashed finger and thumb,
broken a sweet Texas
boy's heart because I'm
impatient, socked
my sister in the eye
with ricochet
and blamed her
for being in my way;
I've failed to build shelter
and pitched tent in my car,
I've left this hammer
in the rain for weeks,
had it stolen and retrieved it,
and once, I gave it
to a long-haired boy
with light eyes and begged
on my knees to get it back;
for the grace, swinging it:
ping of a solid hit
when a word or phrase
sinks its long teeth
in wood, metaphor
grounded in stud—
there are ways
to play a xylophone
with a mallet without
cracking the keys,
but it's the music

of excavation
and demolition I am
wooed by; I can walk
nine blocks to a neighborhood
still sunk and shamed
by Sandy, where
water-stained sheetrock
hosts roaches, where
windows are plywood
doors; this hammer
needs lumber and nails,
concrete and rebar,
it needs hands, it needs
bodies; it won't ever be
enough but it's better
than a rock tossed
or razing a flag;
no, my father wasn't
a carpenter or a blacksmith,
but he knew how
to use his voice
like a bolt of thunder,
and the pictures jumped
from the walls and we
jammed cotton in our ears
and hid among stuffed
animals in our closets
waiting out the storm
that might last for a few
hours or days, rattling
the steel front door,
the basement filling
with water—so I stole
that sound, learned
how to shut someone up
or make them talk, learned
how to rip open a room—

and when the rain
subsided and the wind
died down, we'd venture
outside, survey
the damage, pull
tree limbs from car hoods
and shingles impaled
like crooked tombstones
in the yard, and someone
would get the ladder
and then the work
would start

ANCIENT GRAFFITI

Our first alphabet scratched by copper miners
        in a quarry in Edom: *God, get me out of here.*

Who was here in AD 11? I scrawled *I hate daddy*
        on closet walls when sent for punishment,

and the space suddenly felt a little holy.

When a Fetus Turns to Stone

Rock worn smooth by amniotic waves,
tide of breath: this ectopic love affair.

Chick-like, just hatched then shellacked
in resin, drippy eyes, transparent skin,

a plucked thing. Abdominal molar.
Pestle to grind sorrow in the pelvic bowl.

The heaviest brooch you've ever worn
or carried in the purse of your body.

How still it stays as you wash, toothbrush
the smallest cracks where limbs attach.

No way to chisel its legs loose, the neck
long, to see what went wrong. Though

you might crack it into many lozenge-size
stones that jangle in a pouch. Better yet,

mill to a fine powder, one you sprinkle
over casseroles to serve guests mourning

a loss of their own, a way to share your
grief. Or not. Keep it all to yourself. Snort

the heart-shaped line or spell out its name.
This time the pain in your chest and shortness

of breath will have a root cause, something
to be explained, not this phantom ache.

Five Years of Infertility, Ending with a Child

for Florence, whose name means to blossom

Some things grow better in the dark,
but most flowers will arch their spines

to whatever light they find. Off the path,
a hundred-year sycamore squats, trunk

itself a flash of lightning or a woman
whose hips lie even with knees, torso lifted

toward sky. I'm not a tree. I've not covered
the distance to the moon yet and may not

in this one life. It took five years to plant
the seeds they sent to orbit the moon.

Five years, I clocked my body's tidal forces,
but each month the blood came. I'd spent

my whole life up to that moment not wanting
a child and now this need was all I knew.

Once, in the middle South, I tried to find
the Lost Cove. The pressed clay looked

enough like flesh I understood from where
the old tales came. Every ropy vine in shadow's

crack, a fool snake. In a second cave, I found
a vortex of stones balanced in what must've

been a basin hewn by settlers a century ago,
and beside it, a tub, shaped like an old pram.

If I'd found a child there I'd have taken her
home. In a story I read as a girl, a fishing

woman finds a merchild in a king crab shell
she's hauled after the storm of all storms.

She's righteous enough to consult village
elders, to seek out the sea goddess who fills

the night with her sorrow. Who would return
to me what I'd not yet found? Five years

after they left, the seeds that returned from
the moon were scattered across earth, have

grown full-size. They cast the same shade
and their seeds have become half-moon and

quarter-moon trees. Child, I've carried you
this whole life, just waiting for you to bloom.

IN HER LAP, TO THE WORLD

Once you could send an infant,
under eleven pounds, by post,
trust the carrier to deliver your son—

postage pinned to his little corduroy vest—
to your sister, eighty miles away. It wasn't
legal long. I don't know if I'd prefer

my child to carry a house on her back,
to bite when a hand's too near, or make
a new nest each season. I'm always asking her

to be me and not me, which is what a child is
anyway. Today, everything is soaked.
If I had to make a fire, I'd fail, but I live

with the privilege of not needing to conjure
flame. As I listen to the music of the pond,
I'm sure if I slowed down, I'd know from where

that frog bellows. I might see the whole Earth
breathe. Tell me how to line the path from here
to there with enough obstacles to not wear down

my child when I already know sorrow's great
root is expectation. My friend says you cannot
spoil a child because love cannot cause rot.

I'm hoping she's right, will surrender to this axiom
because I want to be enough. When it's all cloud
should we warn of the storm or let our children name

the few patches of blush and sapphire sky?
Besides this moment, what else can I not replace?

FALLIBLE BEASTS

In the dream, my daughter,
just three, peers at the edge
of the hippo tank and I'm holding
her with the type of grip
most mothers use when hoisting
their sunscreen-slick toddler,
as she leans in, squealing,
but then her weight shifts
and she tips into the tank
and it's high enough that I
cannot swing my leg over
the concrete bulwark, nothing
at my feet to stand on,
which is why I was holding her
in the first place. Their teeth
are not tea-stained marshmallows
and I'm spared the sound, a silent
horror film, this dream, a nightmare
another mother's lived through.

I read the story of the boy mauled
by two jaguars at the Little Rock Zoo,
how the crew used fire extinguishers
to blast the big cats back, though
the black one had bitten the boy's
foot and the yellow his nape.
If we're looking for a causal chain,
here's where Harambe goes down
with a thud. *Oh, Harambe, we love
you get up.* Beautiful beast batting
his eyes and that intelligent stride.

When a team of scientists
and photographers and artists

goes into the Antarctic to study
its majesty, they return from the day's
trek to discover a polar bear
breaking into a tent. They don't kill
the bear because already he's eaten
all of the food (straight through
aluminum cans), exposed film,
dragged an air mattress outside
and shred it to prayer flags.
One man's wounded tone,
as if to say *I trusted you, wild thing,*

and you have abused my trust.
Dear human, even if you've paid
for the land, the single-story house,
you rent this plot from ants. And what
would Harambe's mother, Kayla,
dead a dozen years now, a gas leak
at the Gladys Porter Zoo, what would
she do? Majestic in her own way,
how she stroked her two-year-old's
shoulders and scolded him
in a terribly familiar timbre.

I'd bet my own clapboard house
that she'd kill any man she thought
a threat. You, mother, standing
at the edge of the simulated rainforest,
your fear as real as the scrub grass
at your feet. All mothers
have failed. Sometimes it's a bit
of fiberglass insulation spun
like carnival cotton candy. Five fingers
caught in a car door. My own child bit
by a beach restaurant's pet parrot.
I watched it. She was pretending,
as children do, that she was cooking,

and when she offered the parrot,
high in the rafters, a small plate
of crushed shells and sticks,
he swooped down and chawed
her meaty shin breaking it into blood
bright as the bird's back. The owners
squawked and my daughter cried.
They didn't kill the bird, but each
time we returned, he was caged,
and I was sorry for this, too.

There are things that don't seem
possible, until they are. If we're
taking sides, I'm taking this mother's,
not because I'm a mother who's
failed, or the child of a mother
who's failed too—all of our palm-sized
and glacier failures lined up,
reclaiming the word, which comes
from the Latin *fallere*, which means
to deceive: We want to believe
we can do better, but we too
are wild, fallible beasts.

THE INFANT CORPSES AT THE HOME FOR YOUNG GIRLS

Some stillborn, some born into the still air of dank rooms.
A breed as bad or worse than orphans. I know

why a young mother might kiss her milk-drunk babe
before covering nose and mouth with one hand.

Here, before any man's hurt her, no woman's shamed her,
no god's judged. No way to quell that other hunger: love.

It's pain from the beginning—that inexplicable spasm,
the first time you're kicked from the inside.

THE MOTHER

My last, my least turned most favorite—
though I'll deny it—because if he's a devil
or a god, what could he need from me?

Hadn't I suffered enough, having made
mothering a career, one I didn't want,
but couldn't leave alive. To curse him

unborn, body within my body. He was
part of me, my darkest part—child
of my ill intentions. With a soot-stained

heart, he knew how to fish an eye
from the neighbor's apple-cheeked child.
Son who slipped into night, calling

like some haunted bird tree bound
or the field mouse gripped by death's
groomsman. Guileless, all sinew, the steep

angle of jaw, a type of jaunt and lean
to him. That night, when he hit me,
bit me, thrashed the room, perhaps

I wanted to believe I could free myself
by giving him up. I'd recognize him
in the face of other boys, in the men

my daughters brought home. A little demon
in them all. Even my own face. Especially
as a young girl when I thought I was brave.

3

LEAVING ATLANTIC CITY

In the smog-stained bus terminal, I watch a half-dozen pigeons, peck
along the curb, each a greasy Buddha nodding, absorbed in prayer, feathers
iridescing with the sublime sheen of motor oil on asphalt (black opal
smear, anti-gravity rainbow), a procession through some
invisible labyrinth, one that cannot be lit by infrared or sonar—
resistance, the least of paths—this wandering not aimless, the
503 AC Seasonal sweeps into lot, hiss-kissed air, there
the birds scatter and lift, Ooo-uh sound that seems to burst
from reeds (it has those notes), a call that draws all eyes,
the flock regrouping at the fence (a line) apropos
      three homeless men ask for change—
this is *In God We Trust*. This is the jackpot. This is everyone gets
what they don't want. I am the same, waiting to board, half-shaded
by the overhang. Less and less as I move toward the door, through which
body after body disappears, the faint wail of sirens increasing bayside.
Here, ticket in hand, holding it like some good luck charm
or my last dollar, I look away from the birds, the men, and say this
is what I have earned, I don't owe anyone anything. And if I ask myself
now what I meant. Ask, if I was wrong. It was something I didn't do.

NEW MATH

When solving for
ignorance, X is
a friend
from high school
who writes
Don't be

a criminal and you
won't get killed
When solving
for redemption,
X is pulling
privilege

from its glass case
handing it
the neighborhood kids
zero(s) out
the guilt, where
my guilt

increases
exponentially
over time,
I'd need
a wormhole,
distracts

like the color
green
How many sweaters?
When I Google
"criminal"
stock photos of

white wrists
cuffed, clip art
convicts
dogs behind bars
cursorial animals
adapted to run

long distances
at high speeds
which is to say
they need
to be able to flee
after a $15 markup

the store made
a $400 profit
a hug, a cage
There are ways
to show affection
in the gray sky

of morning
Except here
color isn't irrelevant
Are the unsold
sweaters stained
factory defects

My mother
would say word
problems
should be easy
for me
because they're

stories, but
sometimes
the bully wins
When the constant is
conditional,
I drop my books

grab the swinging
right arm
boy who dated
my cousin
or I run to the nearest
classroom or

I wait to help
the boy [do I tell you

end of hall
knuckles cracking

coward, I stare
praying, which is to say

to roam the halls
in/visible

sirens and bullets,
where I'm

looking for
a solution,

what he looked like?]
pinned against

cheek bone, the way
a t-shirt sucks up

god, stop it, but only
in my head

a Mandelbrot Set of
suffering

a number left or
right of zero

a way to go back to
that boy, the girl

the metal desk
marooned at

blood, but
the constant is

afraid to lose
my privilege

self-same repeating
pattern, equation of

a flag as big as
a king-size bed

I wasn't
in a green sweater.

PUNCH LINE

The joke wishes it wasn't the joke.
It calls a helpline—the joke wants to punch
a bullet through its brow, and it's hard for the operator
to talk the joke down. She says *help is on the way.*

No, don't send the cops. But it's too late. The joke
doesn't have enough pills or a tongue to swallow them.
The joke doesn't have knees to pray. A black man
and a Hispanic are riding in a car. Leave it there.
Leave them in the Sentra at the Quikchek. Let them
drop off their kids at school. Let the cops

bust down the joke's door. Who's driving?
Who the fuck is driving this joke?

> What a relief.
The black man and the Hispanic are both breathing, cuffed
upright in the back of a cruiser. No blood on the cop's hands.

Let's make you the cop. Let's make you the law.
What sound does a body make when it's in a chokehold?

A black cop is driving his Hispanic partner. A white cop
is driving himself crazy. He's tired of telling the same group
of young men to stop loitering on the platform. Every night,
just milling around, blocking people, pushing, shoving
each other, a game, intimidating passengers.

Today you're the black man. You've read the script, memorized
your lines *Yes, officer* perfected the least intimidating pitch,
a walk that won't draw attention, should you enter
a convenience store, a bank.

The car is driving itself. The car is the joke.
The tires smoke and the brakes sink to the floorboard.

Two cops are in a car—this one isn't a joke (turns out
the first one wasn't either)—parked, gunned down.
As if these young men's deaths will bring another
back to his children. Some illogical exchange
fallen angels run.

                    A black car, driving rain,
eye whites, night, the drawbridge of gritted teeth opening,
no such thing as bullet-proof words, floodlight, that
deer stare, the moment before a buck turns, threatened,
having done nothing.

              This joke is a loaded Glock 19.

Between box spring and mattress, in the glove box.
A siren wails. Two cops sit in a car. Two cops die in a car.
This isn't a joke. This was supposed to be a joke.
We were supposed to laugh and say *Oh, that's not right*
and shake our heads and go on with our days, all of us—
black man, Hispanic, cop, you, reader, sitting there
waiting for the punch line, the big haha aha.

Maybe you're saying *No, that's not funny* or
It's true, you know. Maybe you're telling the joke.

When the cops arrive the joke is sobbing. The joke asks
to be locked up. It won't tell itself anymore. It wants
a new punch line. It wants to reform itself, to be
elegy for cop, black man, his panic.

WEST OF PERTH

I, too, have wanted to disappear,
dissolve, a powdered mix in cold milk,
chilled to set. Guests won't know

what's on their tongues, what tastes
so good or foul. What might they say:
Two days straight of rain. Have they found

the plane? In other news, a missing boy washed
up in the bay. To slip through thin ice:
a trapdoor you're waiting for, the chute

that never ends, headlong into the dark
brackish intercostal waterway, so cold
it ceases to smell like salt, so cold it cuts skin.

&

On the flight home from Delhi, I watched
the seatback screen trace the flight's arc over
continent and ocean. How often I ignored

the attendants' evacuation warning. I was too busy
wanting to go home and wanting to leave a life
I was already living.

&

Still no sign of the Boeing triple 7,
five days now since the plane vanished.
I imagine a stewardess taking

cocktail orders, passing single-serve Ritz
down the rows. Earlier, a lecture
on inflatable rafts, floatation seat cushions.

When the plastic bag descends, secure
your own mask first. Perhaps the shades
are drawn and everyone settles

for a nap. The faint blue glow of televisions
lulling weary passengers. Is it possible
the plane is still airborne, as in the movies

when another plane meets it at a certain altitude
to refuel, so that it might continue without
touching down? Perhaps it will land

at LAX at noon, each passenger waiting
by the baggage carousel, an infant howling
for milk. I know the ocean's an unreasonable

negotiator, so let's not think about cabin pressure
or a fire onboard. Instead, a neat splash
off the high dive. If only a humpback whale

should arrive, open its mouth, inviting every
water-logged passenger onto the red carpet
of its tongue, the teeth, like so many ergonomic

benches for the weary to lie upon. This wishful
thinking at listless wit's end. Nowhere to place
a roadside memorial. A garland of peonies on a buoy.

DISAPPEARING LADY

To run from the every day collapse,
its chain-link and water torture tank.
A woman like a wisp of cloud, lunula

of nail. She halves herself again.
If a black hole is a dead star,
how does it die? For her next trick,

balanced on icepick—a bag of flour
to cake. No yellow wallpaper here.
She's a stitch of floss, drawing blood.

The unpaved road, dirt lot. The same
dream on hands and knees. A contortion
gone wrong: trying to hang herself

with her own hair. This woman can fit
so many things between her legs. Hurry.
We all die so slowly, then all at once.

PARABLE: HOW TO ESCAPE THE GENERAL INSIDE

Disappear, again. No white knight. Covered heads under cover
     of night's starless steed, unbridled city quiet under occupation
     (Mosul at night)—
                    a dozing cabbie, a veil—
     no ghost of ISIS past or future to swoop in and carry you away.
That day: you disappeared from homes and village, were divvied up
     like livestock: separated into young and old, pretty and not pretty,
     the only criteria for a wife.

     If he is a general, and they're not all generals,
     though they wish to be, you must ask
     for a bigger house, one with Venetian blinds
     and a western toilet. He'll give you what you want
     because he wants you to treat him
     like the general inside him.
                    But once you're in
     the big house, once you're mourning—having asked
     for your forty days—you'll need a room for all your grief,
     You've taken off your rings and covered your hair.
     This house will not do either. Tell him.

Your tongue is long, he says, *don't talk until I'm finished or I will cut it out.*

     Toronto Metro: "Yazidi woman made a daring escape but her
     12-year-old daughter remains 'married' to ISIS fighter"; *Inquisitr*:
     "ISIS sends horrific rape and torture video to parents: daughters'
     body parts left on doorstep"; *Christian Today*: "More ISIS atrocities
     surface: 250 women executed for refusing 'sexual jihad'"; *The CNN
     Freedom Project*: "'Hundreds' of Yazidi women killing themselves in
     ISIS captivity."

You watch your own kin cut herself
     with a bit of window glass. No place is safe.
     He must believe he's smarter than you are.

Talk too much and you and your sisters will be beaten,
split up, restrained with electrical tape, raped,
      which is to say,

                your new marriage will be consecrated,
                which is not to say, you have lost.

Instead of fear, show dissatisfaction,
that you're unimpressed, that if you're the wife of a general,
you should have a gas range, room to entertain.
You move again—until you find a wooden door, the balcony,
a key, the grand escape: some honest do-gooder who's secured
fake ids, helped you and your four sisters flee.

          Remember, it is a single-use escape hatch.
The generals are back in the village, choosing new girls.
      They'll beat them all this time and split up sisters.
      No negotiation, no western house. They will be lucky
to keep their names. How can a general trust another
      girl after you lied to him? He will show everyone
      that the general is smarter: he will clamp down his fist.
She will bear him a son. Or he's not done yet.

THE GRAND OPERA OF BOKO HARAM

after Henry Reed's "Naming of Parts"

Here's where the instruments of torture break into song. Earlier,
an open cargo truck, a skulk of men in sweat-stained fatigues.
And later, we shall have what to do after the rapes. But here, here
the instruments of torture break into song. Doe-eyed girls
in plaits learn algebra on handheld slates, solve for x and y,
     and the instruments of torture break into song.

An eyeless machete rears up on its handle. Its blade
is a Cheshire grin. A chorus line of leggy grenades
palms safeties, upturns jowly Buddha faces,
which implies a compassion they have not got. If we add
zero to any number, we will end up with the same number,
     which implies a stability we have not got.

No gossip's brindle or iron maiden where a pair of scissors
or hot coals will do. And please do not let me see anyone
using his finger. You can convert the girls quite easily,
watch the smallest start to weep. A peddler sells twice
as many pears in the afternoon after letting everyone
     touch any of them using their fingers.

And this you can see is a whip, with a voice for soprano
arias. Hear how the notes turn steel-blue block walls
and concrete slab to calm seas, cloudless sky: we call this
a cappella. Calm seized. Clouds sigh. We must be careful
not to make mistakes when dealing with negative signs:
     they call it Deus ex Machina.

They call it the finale: it is quite easy
when the smallest starts to weep: like the whip,
and the barrel's open mouth, and the blade and burnt house,
which implies a hope we have not got; and the location
of the girls is unknown: halfway between sea and sky,
     they're instruments of torture, broken song.

THIS BOMB CAN'T RETURN TO SENDER

The manila envelope is a map a window. The silver plane clip that closes
has closed this bit of air mail delivered the news a sudden explosion smoke
mirrored screams ash. We're dropping bags of rice bundles of poems
that might start fires clog gutters streets sewage backs up. The world

doesn't need so many words no return address this bomb can't return
to sender undisclosed recipients a mass mailing this murder ink smeared
rain-soaked package left on doorstep someone else's paper waterlogged
circulars prom photos a birth a death certificate the clippings
my mother-in-law sends of hurricanes.

           Hard to believe this comes from the sky because the earth
erupts with a force so violent it must've come from within. Always
the smudged glass of Hiroshima the World Trade Center's gutted core
Cairo Tunisia Beirut... a pair of shoes or blood-spattered pavement one

end of a jump rope's frayed edges the other pink handle perfectly intact.
This isn't a south Florida sinkhole. This isn't a tsunami along the Pacific
Rim. This is a direct order a man in a plane a man flying a drone. This
is a missile manufactured in Texas Chechnya Jiangsu Province.

This is airmail a first-class tragedy licked and sealed the last letter I wrote
or the one I didn't send a girl's blue shoe one half of a jump rope. This is all
that's left. This map of before the dream after. That little clip holding
the envelope closed inside the envelope the envelope please. Please.

MORE OR LESS AMERICAN

Riding the L into Brooklyn	toeing the thin line between friendly and	crazy— I tip my chin toward
a man with gray-green eyes	a voice as warm as water beneath	the bridge he says *you're*
not from here that choke of panic	every answer wrong, but I say	*from Jersey* and he says
That's not what I mean	this very moment or maternity ward	*No, as in America*
I look for hidden camera	someone with a mic to slap my shoulder	what's it like to be profiled
or maybe he's reading my mind	a vodka ad with lean models	high cheekbones, flawless skin
I don't know what it is to be	this country, couldn't convince myself	give up its luxuries: so much bread
stale on shleves unless	there's a storm the half-truth of	every sale, and where, the tap's clean
I ask *where are you from?*	*not here* he says, exiting	at Court Street some midday sage
heading above the bowels of NY	leaving me with beat-boxing	break boy eating bible verse before
unveiling a belch veil of exhaustion	questions my head, this face	others wear my mother's tired eyes

ANGEL OF ASSASSINATION

after Charlotte Corday

When Legros slapped her severed head,
the crowd mistook her blush: not shame
but disgust. A simple man to think the just-

dead do not judge. If her tongue still flapped,
she'd spit Plutarch's credo. To slice Brie
de Meaux or a man's aorta, best to whet

the six-inch blade of a woman's spite
so blood pours freely as Merlot, stains the tub.
Heart of terror put to bed, a bust of marble cut.

The men we fear were born from mortal wombs.
Apt for a lady executioner: immigrant cook
or one of the wives we think too dumb

to give a fuck in simple flats, dressed
in black. She doesn't need to love death
(to do the deed), just life enough and liberty.

4

A GUIDE FOR SOUVENIRS YOU GET WITHOUT GOING ON THE TRIP

Pardon our noise. It's the sound of freedom.
    –Cherry Point Marine Corp Air Station

I was born in Cherry Point, North Carolina,
and I was not sexually experienced, couldn't

tell you the cherry's point, which end of stem
or how a limbic tongue ties knots. That almost

arm from branch to bud or fruit, an arboretum's
umbilicalis. On base, muscled engines chant

takeoff takeoff takeoff. Mother swells, cerise
cheeked, la linea negra a prime meridian

from navel to labia, she's ready to split. Inside
the cherry's thin skin, a merlot, juice of a drupe

so small. In the trailer's white walls, cockroaches
climb the studs, fuck furiously in the dark.

The lining up and moving out. The wooden seed,
a skull. At roll call, tight-assed boys from Sioux City,

Philadelphia, Tampa cry out name and rank, sir,
yes, sir. What's the point?—the tip, the fleshy head?

Ooh Rah! It's pump and thrust, it's rolled sleeves
and crisp cuffs, crew cuts, dog tags clacking

sternums, the music of the machine roars on.
The cherry on top: another girl in the world.

TAYLOR SWIFT AND HER WIN-A-BAGEL WINNEBAGO

The joke's on me. No blonde. Her glossy, cream cheese-
colored RV flashing neon, "Shake it Off" roaring
from the far end of the Walmart parking lot. Instead

of tossing tank tops and lip-gloss, she wants to feed
her fans some doughy concoction that'll fill their guts,
undercut heartbreak's hunger: the *1989* special

with strawberry spread. I was eight then, long hair,
lip-syncing Madonna's "Like a Prayer," down
on my knees with a Conair brush, wanting to be

the beauty queens my cousins were, wishing
for breasts full and heavy as bagels. Oh Taylor,
swift us to paradise where a girl can eat her carb's

content. Like once in that Rutgers parking lot,
Erykah Badu's "Bag Lady" blaring from the small
horn mounted atop the red and gold diner car, as if

it was Girls' Day Out at the grease truck compound.
We were looking for our trophies having made it
through the night unscathed, no man's prisoner,

no small meal would do, only the blessed mother
of fat sandwiches. From my bra strap, I pulled
crumpled bills damp with sweat, and the queen cook,

a silk scarf covering her braids, gave me a knowing nod,
like one who has been on the all-night trek and passed
through the gates to safety, to this promised land

of grease and meat and cheese. Each wearing our
own crown of sweat curls, a day-old sheen upon
our brows, my sisters and I waited for subs the size

of sneakers to arrive in their checkered cardboard
boats. And that first bite—all-beef burger slathered
in red sauce, mozza, long hots, and topped with

steak fries—burst in my mouth, marinara oozing
from jowls. We licked the juice between our rings,
running down wrists, victorious in our quest to be fed.

THE TREED LADY

When the boy in my Bible class planted a wad
of Bazooka Joe at the root of my skull, he didn't

expect a sapodilla to grow. Wrist-thick trunk
tangled in tresses overnight, white sap gumming

cotton sheets, my lilac pajama sleeves. Smell
of something sweet, green—not grass or home

of the original mango. A miracle for having
forgiven this boy for putting his hands on me,

no penitence for his trespass in the garden
of my hair. Another tree of knowledge to press

my crown into. Though ruffians teased, would
pin me down, dig nails into the bark banking

my neck, pull sap until it snapped. My new
thirst unimaginable. But there are ways to live

with the gifts we've been given: I cast shade
wherever I picnic, and as the fruits sag heavy

from the upper boughs, I can shake my head,
release their tender yield. As when the sap slips

viscous down my back, my lover scrapes it clean
with a plastic spatula, and we chew for hours.

BEWARE, BEWARE

a quotilla after Plath's "Lady Lazarus"

Out of practice, the body convinces the mind this desert
of want is love. It took me so long to learn my type:
the evening of his eyes starless, lit only by my face;
ash trailing desire's reckless comet. If he's vulnerable
I am dangerous—the opposite of wounded isn't healed. Promises
rise along the stretch of stomach from hip crease to navel
with morning's first ochre smear. This throbbing
my younger self mistook. A woman in a red dress changes
red [firecracker/pinot noir]. I roam on all fours—lips and
hair ripen when brushed—trail the ones who want to be loved
and touched just as much. But it will never be enough:
I know psalms that draw sailors to rocks, I've watched sirens
eat men gripping oarlocks. Beware: the shiver is not from the cold.
Men, when night's hot breath unstrings the necklace of my spine,
like any first kiss or the moment before a cum cry, I become the
air. Go ahead, try to survive without me.

VENTRILOQUISM FOR DUMMIES

Oh, I did most of it wrong, having been
the puppet so long—a childhood parroting
truisms I pushed around my dinner plate.

It was hard to jam my fist inside, but then
I knew how one could say it fit like a glove.
Though how to pick from my secret selves,

or a single face to match its form. That voice
inside—like and unlike the one on my tongue—
a child buried between my ribs? A limbo-

locked auntie settling her tithe? A dormant
volcano? The instructor advised practice
at home, as I did as a teen—gritting teeth

and throwing my voice against slammed
doors or the shower's heavy hush. Alone,
I'd hold a finger to my mouth as if warning

of an infant asleep on the couch. It's hard
to force air deep within the throat (pretend
to cough) or through your nose. A lipless

alphabet is seven letters short; substitute
"ooh" for "w," "da" or "geh" for "b."
Dear slack-jaw dummy with a deviated

septum: I cannot convince myself that you
or I am completely alive. There, there. I'll
stroke your silken hair and hum our favorite

Beatles tune. Listen to us: a tractor-trailer
jack-knifes on the snow-slick pass and a Pinto
skids toward it. My lips are snow, yours the pass.

WHAT LIES BEYOND RESCUE

Spent rocket stages, paint flakes
and frozen coolant in Earth's low orbit.
Ed White's lost glove gathering speed.

An eye that's scratched beyond repair.
The thing that's gone too far past
a sink's drain hatch, though a friend

retrieved his son's stuffed humpback
who'd fallen in the open sewer cap.
Cake that's slid from plate, rhomboid

icing floor. Maybe I'd serve a slice
cut from its untouched upper half,
perfectly formed and free of dust and fur.

The rest: scraps for worms. Sometimes
when a car's totaled, it'll still run, bent
axle and dripping fuel, unsalvageable vessel—

a body swollen with tumor—
the mind clicks on
bright human whirling to life.

LEAVES OF PAPER, SHARDS OF BONE

Today I find a spell on a leaf of paper
tucked in an old book: prescription
for how to lift sorrow from bones.

If I could dial back to when I'd run
for hours, when it was enough to spin
in late afternoon's tawny light,

to take another's hand and tell a secret
in a loud voice. I was almost free then.
There was some small chance I might fly

if I leaned into the air around me.
I believed I could save something that
needed saving by laying my palms on it.

THE EARTH IS A SOLAR-POWERED JUKEBOX

In the late afternoon of siesta,
I hear the farmers' horses up the hill,
the suck and pull of wet earth on hooves.
A fog of black flies hovers by eyes and along
thin spines; ears twitch and tails flick
like small brooms sweeping the air.
A mile away, the Atlantic pounds the coast,
cashmere waves thump the shoreline
and offshore winds bend scrubby trees
toward surf. Their leaves flutter
like tiny leather castanets filling the air
with a song I've heard a million times before.

ᥱᴼ

I complained to my friend this morning
about the music the news uses to cut
between segments, to dramatize the wait
for the jury's response in the murder case.
Imagine the soundscape that night. How fear
distorts (or sharpens) the senses: loose change
or a dragging chain, the heavy footfall
of girls jumping rope, ice or glass breaking
by the stairs. How many mornings have I woken
doubled over with longing, laundry snapping
on the line outside my window?

ᥱᴼ

Once, just after sunrise, I heard a woman's voice
rise up to meet the wind's tune in high grass.
I threw open the dormers and stuck my head out.
No houses nearby, no woman walking
the mountain pass or through the fields below.
I imagine short hair framing a plain face,
dark brown eyes, a long corridor

in which I enter, walk, the night sky
in the Himalayas, an empty truck stop,
the split ribs of a doe in a ravine.
In the distance, the clatter of wheels
on tracks, a conductor pulls the whistle,
putting his own signature on the air.
A huge lasso, the train gathers
the whole landscape and brings it back
to me so that I know exactly where I am.

WHAT IS THERE TO BE LEARNED

Whenever I listen to Billie Holiday, I am reminded
of that Levis poem and how we sat in the back room
of the library, just out of reach, box fan blowing the heat

between us. I'd like to believe that I'd know what to save
in a fire, children first, the cat. I might want my mother's
rings, my good pillow. It's hard to tell what I keep closest

to my heart and how it gets there. That bright night
I drove to your end of the island, nerves sparking, afraid
my car would die on your block or be broken into. Maybe

it was a way to convince myself it would be only a kiss,
first on the street, and then, on the edge of your bed, where
I held your hand, then ran fingers through your hair

for hours. It's not appropriate to imagine a house in flames
when others have stood in the street and watched decades
collapse. But I have always imagined the end of days.

If I am honest with myself I love the way a substation
sounds like the ocean. Today the clouds look like x-rays
of a fractured skull and I understand wanting to stand

in the middle of the track, to jump from the trestle.
Like Levis and Holiday, like you, I'd like to make some
dignity out of loneliness, and if I keep using the conditional

there's a chance it'll happen, right? In my throat, barbed
wire coils, and meaning drags itself over, pant leg caught,
blood at its heels. I have not become whoever I will become,

but this is who I am now, and it is all I can offer. What I'm
trying to say is: in July when the irrigation guns grew hot
enough to seal an eye shut, I was most afraid of myself.

NOTES

Toddler Pulled from Rubble in Aleppo references the video recording of two-year-old Rani Halil's rescue after an air strike blast in Aleppo on December 16, 2013.

Five Years of Infertility, Ending with a Child references the moon tree on the University of the South's campus—a tree grown from one of the 500 seeds Stuart Roosa took with him during the Apollo 14 mission in 1971.

Leaving Atlantic City is a palimpsest of Jorie Graham's "Prayer."

Punch Line is in memory of Michael Brown, Eric Garner, Alton Sterling, Philando Castile, and the hundreds of men, women, and children of color who have been murdered and/or terrorized by police.

West of Perth pays tribute to the passengers and crew of Malaysia Airlines Flight 370 and Kennedy Rios of Ventnor, NJ.

Parable: How to Escape the General Inside honors the Yazidi women who have escaped their captors and those who are still living in captivity.

The Grand Opera of Boko Haram pays homage to the female students kidnapped from the Government Secondary School in Chibok, Nigeria.

This Bomb Can't Return to Sender is in memory of the innumerable innocents lost to war and is after Sarah Van Sanden's "Seed on Envelope" (Graphite and Conté crayon on manila envelope, 11" x 6").

Acknowledgments

Infinite gratitude to the editors of the following journals in which these poems first appeared, some in slightly different form or under different titles:

APIARY	West of Perth
The Collagist	Where Does the Rabbit Go When the Hounds Are Loosed?
Compose	Little Black Dress The Mother
Connotation Press: An Online Artifact	Fallible Beasts Parable: How to Escape the General Inside The Treed Lady
Cutthroat	The Jinxed Bullet Catch Where Mermaids Come From
The FEM	Playing the Husband
Glass: A Journal of Poetry	On the Cave Wall, the Great Black Bird Carries a Girl Into the Sky When a Fetus Turns to Stone
HEArt	The Grand Opera of Boko Haram
Hot Metal Bridge	More or Less American
Jet Fuel Review	The Infant Corpses at the Home for Young Girls This Bomb Can't Return to Sender Toddler Pulled from Rubble in Aleppo

Opossum	Taylor Swift and Her Win-a-Bagel Winnebago
Ovunque Siamo	In Her Lap, to the World Ode to Afterthought What Lies Beyond Rescue
Passages North	A Guide for Souvenirs You Get Without Going on the Trip
Pith	Ancient Graffiti
Pittsburgh Poetry Review	When I Was the Diving Girl
The Prague Revue	Leaving Atlantic City
The Raleigh Review	The White Horses of Wainui Beach
RHINO	Disappearing Lady
Salamander	Who Hasn't Hoarded One Milky Stone in a Deep Pocket?
Smartish Pace	The Earth Is a Solar-Powered Jukebox
Southern Humanities Review	Punch Line
Split Lip	New Math Un-Naming a Thing
Waxwing	Five Years of Infertility, Ending with a Child What Is There to be Learned

Thanks as well to the editors of *Jet Fuel Review* for nominating "The Infant Corpses at the Home for Young Girls" for a Pushcart Prize and Best of the Net; the judges of the 2013 Bellauh Rose Poetry Prize for naming "The Earth Is a Solar-Powered Jukebox" second place; the judges of the 2017 Elinor Benedict Poetry Prize for selecting "A Guide for Souvenirs You Get Without Going on the Trip," as the winner; the judges of the 2016 Woodrow Hall Top Shelf Award for selecting "The Grand Opera of Boko Haram" as the winner; and the judges of the 2016 Auburn Witness Poetry Prize for selecting "Punch Line" as the winner.

Unending thanks to those who have helped and held me and these poems. Thank you, first readers and writing friends—Cynthia Arrieu-King, Erica Bodwell, Barbara Daniels, Joel Dias-Porter, Gail Dimaggio, Gianni Gaudino, Peter Murphy, Nancy Reddy, & Emily Van Duyne. Thank you, SJ Poets Collective, World Above, & Murphy Writing family for community and encouragement. Thank you, students, colleagues, and other friends, who challenge me to be a smarter, better human.

Thank you, Allison Joseph and Agape Editions for believing in this book. Fox Frazier-Foley and Jasmine An, thank you for treating me and these poems with so much love and care.

Thank you to Colrain Manuscript Conference, Firefly Farms, Rivendell Writers' Colony, Stockton University, and Tupelo Press' 30/30 Project for fellowship, time, and solitude.

Thank you, friends and family for helping to keep my family together each time I went away to write. Thank you, AJ, for believing in me and my poetry, for the gift of time, for the love and stability necessary to write these poems. Thank you, thieves in a white getaway car, for offering perspective and for forcing me to start the next project, this book.

Thank you to those who have shared your own survival with me. Thank you to those brave writers and humans, in whose footsteps I follow, who have been/are writing and working to heal and for change. May these poems, in some small way, honor what we have lost.

CPSIA information can be obtained
at www.ICGtesting.com
Printed in the USA
BVHW092202120222
628885BV00004B/105